SPACE

Scientific Consultant:
Amy Gallagher
Hayden Planetarium
American Museum of Natural History

Photo credits:
Bettman Archives, Pages 7-8, 14, 20
Daily Telegraph, Page 13
Gamma Liaison, Pages 15, 25, 28
Gamma Liaison/ NASA, Pages 19, 24
Monique Salaber/Gamma Liaison, Page 15
Susan Greenwood/ Gamma Liaison, Page 15
B. Markel/ Gamma Liaison, Pages 16-17
International Stock, Pages 14-15, 19-20, 24
Mark Newman/ International Stock, Page 16
NASA/ Associated Press, Page7
NASA, Pages 7, 10-11, 13-15, 18, 20-24
NASA/ International Stock, Pages 9, 11, 16, 18
UPI/ Bettman/ NASA, Page 12
UPI/ Bettman, Page 25
Wide World Photos, 6-13,15-23, 28, 29

Illustrations:
Howard S. Friedman — Endpage; Pages 6-7, 17, 22, 26-27

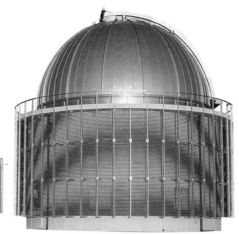

Copyright © 1996
Kidsbooks, Inc.
3535 West Peterson Avenue.
Chicago, IL 60659

Printed in Canada.

EYES ON ADVENTURE™

EXPLORING
SPACE

Written by
Leigh Hope Wood

kidsbooks®
Incorporated

INTO SPACE

Our world seems very large, but Earth represents an incredibly small place in the universe. Outside our planet is the rest of our solar system, which is contained within the Milky Way galaxy. If you could travel at the speed of light, 186,000 miles per second, it would take you 100,000 years to cross the Milky Way. And beyond it is the rest of the universe—billions and billions of other galaxies.

SHAPELY GALAXIES ▲

Galaxies have shape. The Milky Way is spiral shaped, like a whirlpool. Some galaxies are *elliptical*, or oval shaped. In this photo, many galaxy shapes and colors can be seen. The photo, taken by the Hubble Telescope, is the deepest view we've ever had of the universe.

▼ A spiral galaxy.

THE WANDERERS

Planets are always moving, revolving around the Sun. The ancient Greeks named these restless objects *planets*, which means wanderers. Today we know of nine in our solar system—Mercury, Venus, Earth, Mars, Jupiter, Saturn, Uranus, Neptune, and Pluto. Moons also "wander," or revolve, around their planet.

SOLAR CENTER

For a long time, people believed the Earth to be at the center of all heavenly bodies. Then, in the fifteenth century, a Polish monk named Copernicus suggested that the Sun was at the center. People were shocked by this theory.

SKY LIGHTS

For your first space adventure, look into the night sky. Even without the aid of a telescope, you can see our Moon, the five planets closest to us, and more than 5,000 stars. You can even see the glow from another galaxy, called Andromeda.

GRAVITY GLUE

Ever wonder what holds our solar system together? Isaac Newton figured out the answer. An attraction, or pull, which he called *gravity* keeps the planets circling, or *orbiting*, the Sun. If it weren't for the gravity between the Sun and planets, the planets might move through space in a straight line. Also, Earth's gravity is what holds you to the ground.

▲ This color-enhanced picture of the Moon was taken by the *Galileo* spacecraft, which was named for the great astronomer. Blue and orange shades indicate volcanic lava flows.

THE GREAT GALILEO

Known as the father of experimental science, Galileo Galilei was the first scientist to test his theories. In astronomy, he was the first to use the telescope to study space. He identified four moons of Jupiter and described our Moon's surface as rugged and mountainous. His discoveries caused scientists to think of planets as being worlds like our own Earth.

MINOR PLANETS

There are also jagged and round chunks of rock known as *asteroids* revolving around the Sun. These are minor planets, and there are thousands of them located between the orbits of Mars and Jupiter in an asteroid "belt." But some are outside the belt and sometimes pass very near to Earth.

UP, UP, AND AWAY!

It's only human to want to explore other worlds. Scientists started out viewing space from the ground, and telescopes brought them a little closer to other planets. But some people dreamed of actually going there. That's how space travel began.

A science-fiction book that really inspired early rocket scientists was Jules Verne's *From the Earth to the Moon*, published in the 19th century.

STEP ROCKETS ▲

In 1926, Robert H. Goddard became the first to build and launch a liquid-fuel rocket, which traveled 184 feet. He also created the "step" rocket. As fuel was used up in one stage, that section of the rocket would be dropped. It was one of the most significant inventions for getting rockets beyond the gravity of Earth.

◀ SHORT FLIGHT

The U.S. had trouble getting a *satellite* into space. Satellites are objects or vehicles launched into space to orbit the Earth. One called the *Vanguard* was ignited for launch in 1957, but the rocket rose only four feet, fell back to the launch pad, and exploded.

8

RACE IN SPACE

Rocket science really advanced during World War II. After the war, both the U.S. and the Soviet Union began taking steps toward getting into space. On October 4, 1957, when the Soviets launched a rocket carrying the satellite called *Sputnik* I, an all-out space race began.

Early U.S. space capsule. ▶

The *Sputnik* I satellite.

DOG'S DAY ▶

Four weeks after *Sputnik* I was sent to space, the Soviets launched a satellite carrying a dog named Laika. The purpose was to study the effects of the flight on a live animal. It was clear to the U.S. that the Soviets were preparing to send people into space.

Yuri Gagarin was the first man in space.

LEAVING EARTH

When the Soviets sent an unmanned ship to orbit the Moon, it sent back pictures. The world was stunned. Next, the Soviets launched the first man into space, then the first woman. The Soviets were also the first to perform a *spacewalk*—when an astronaut goes outside his or her ship.

Among these *Mercury* astronauts, John Glenn stands second from the right in the first row. ▶

ONE STEP CLOSER

The U.S. *Gemini* missions paved the way for landing an astronaut on the Moon. During one mission, astronaut Edward H. White became the first American to space-walk.

▲ Edward White walking in space.

GROUPING THE TROOPS

In 1958, President Eisenhower created a government agency to organize space exploration—the *National Aeronautics and Space Administration* (NASA). The organization's Mercury project finally put an American into space, when John Glenn orbited the Earth on February 20, 1962.

MAN ON THE MOON

Up until the 1960s, the Moon was an unknown world, and people had seen it only at a great distance, about 240,000 miles away. Then the United States' Apollo 11 mission landed there. The whole world got a close-up picture of the gigantic craters and rocky surface of the lunar landscape.

ON THE DARK SIDE OF THE MOON

The lunar module called the *Eagle* landed on the dark side of the Moon on July 16, 1969. Neil Armstrong emerged, stepped down a ladder to the Moon's surface, and said, "That's one small step for [a] man, one giant leap for mankind."

▲ The *Apollo* 11 blastoff.

EASY DOES IT

Walking on the Moon is fairly easy, but it's bouncy. Gravity is one-sixth of what it is on Earth, and things seem to weigh that much less. If you weigh 100 pounds on Earth, you'd weigh about 16 pounds on the Moon. The *Apollo* astronauts felt light and bobbed along as they explored.

◀ Scientists at NASA had feared that astronauts would have to wade through several feet of Moon dust just to get around. But footprints proved there was only a fraction of an inch of this powdery soil.

SPLASHDOWN

Once the Moon work was complete, the *Eagle* met up with the command module *Columbia*. For the next 60 hours, the spaceship traveled home. It entered Earth's atmosphere in a shower of fire at 25,000 miles per hour, before splashing down in the Pacific.

Apollo 11 astronauts were given a ticker-tape parade in New York City to welcome them home.

MISSION CONTROL ▼

Mission controllers on the ground communicate with astronauts millions of miles away from Earth.

MOON BUGGY

Just two years after the first landing, a car was brought along to the Moon, the *Apollo 15 Rover*. This battery-powered buggy had tires made of piano wires. Although practically weightless—about 76 pounds on the Moon—it really dug into the lunar dust.

LUNAR LABOR

Part of the astronauts' mission was to collect rock and soil for study back home. With no organisms having ever been found, the Moon is said to be a "dead planet." But it's an *old*, dead planet. Rock collected by Apollo 15 astronauts proved to be about four billion years old!

NEW DIRECTIONS

The success of the Apollo missions encouraged NASA to make more plans for space exploration. Among them were plans to build a space station and a shuttle. Another goal was to send unmanned probes to explore other planets.

▲ Astronaut Sally K. Ride, the first U.S. woman in space, made a flight on the *Challenger* in 1983.

▲ *Skylab* offered the first shower in space.

▲ EYES IN THE SKY

After the Moon landing, NASA launched *Skylab*. This station floating in space would allow greater observations of the Sun, which can't be viewed directly with the human eye. Also, it would provide clearer images of stars. Out in space beyond the wavering gases of Earth's atmosphere, stars don't appear to twinkle.

FIRST FLIGHT

The shuttle was a masterpiece of engineering. After being launched into space by a rocket, it could be flown and landed like a plane. In 1981, *Columbia* was the first shuttle to make a space flight. 12

UNMANNED PROBES

NASA has launched many unmanned ships to explore space. These probes are less expensive. They also expand our knowledge of space without endangering human life. Between 1969 and 1978, 13 *Pioneer*, *Mariner*, *Viking* and *Voyager* probes were shot into space. In 1996, the *Galileo* probe landed on Jupiter.

◀ PAYLOAD

The shuttle was designed to transport equipment as well as astronauts into space. Its total payload could weigh up to 65,000 pounds. In 1990, it carried and released the Hubble Space Telescope. This orbiting telescope provides clear pictures of stars, planets, and other heavenly bodies.

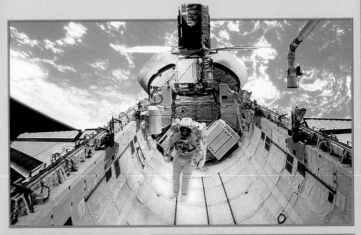

REPAIR CREW ▶

One very important job done by shuttle crews is repair work. A robotic arm on the shuttle helps bring satellites into the cargo bay. The first satellite repair work was done in 1984 to the *Solar Max*. George D. "Pinky" Nelson and James D. "Ox" Van Hoften repaired the astronomy satellite and released it back into orbit.

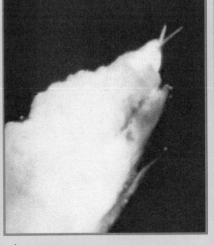

HUMAN SATELLITE

With one new high-tech piece of equipment, a couple of astronauts became the first human satellites. In 1984, the *Manned Maneuvering Unit* (MMU) allowed astronauts Bruce McCandless and Robert Stewart to do a spacewalk without being attached to the ship. McCandless flew 320 feet from the *Challenger*.

▲ MISSION OF DISASTER

The space shuttle was incredibly reliable for 24 flights. Then, on January 28, 1986, the *Challenger* exploded ninety seconds into its flight, killing seven crew members. The tragedy was heart-stopping, and reminded the public how dangerous space exploration can sometimes be.

LOOKING TOWARD HOME

At the time of the first Moon landing, space was considered the final frontier—the place where new worlds would be discovered. No one really imagined the impact space technology would have back on Earth. Today, it's hard to imagine living *without* satellites.

In 1962, *Telstar* I became the first active communications satellite. It also transmitted the first live television broadcast across the Atlantic.

EASY LISTENING

Satellites have made communication between continents easier and faster. In 1956, voice cable laid across the bottom of the ocean could only handle 36 phone calls at a time. Today, the most advanced international satellites can carry more than 120,000 calls at a time.

Some satellites remain stationary in space, while others orbit the Earth.

FIRE DOWN BELOW

Earth-survey satellites watch the environment. They measure quantities of water and ice, monitor coastal water pollution, and evaluate soil. When there's a fire in the forest, these satellites will detect it.

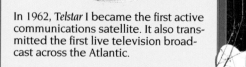

DISH CITY

Today, more than 3 million Americans have satellite dishes that pick up television transmissions. Dishes are also used by broadcast stations, which transmit information to satellites.

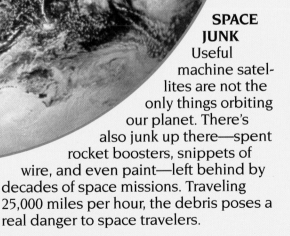

▼ When space photos showed a royal blue sphere suspended in space like a jewel, Earthlings got a new view of their own planet.

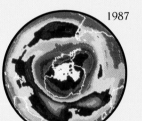

HURRICANE HUGO
31. 4N 78. 4W
21 SEPT 135 MPH

KILLER STORM ▲

On the news at night, weather broadcasters often show pictures of cloud patterns moving across the Earth. These satellite photos help predict rain, snow, and severe storms. Hurricane Hugo was one of the most powerful storms of the century. But it killed only 40 people, because satellites gave residents an early warning.

1987

1988

◀ GLOBAL WARMING

Earth's atmosphere is composed of five layers of gases that surround the planet. They block much of the Sun's radiation. However, holes have developed in the ozone layer because of Earth's pollution. The two satellite images at left compare the size of the holes in 1987 and 1988.

SPACE JUNK

Useful machine satellites are not the only things orbiting our planet. There's also junk up there—spent rocket boosters, snippets of wire, and even paint—left behind by decades of space missions. Traveling 25,000 miles per hour, the debris poses a real danger to space travelers.

THE ULTIMATE MAP ▶

Want to find a stolen car, detect an oil leak in an ocean tanker, or determine the quickest route to your destination? The *Global Positioning System* (GPS) can do it for you. This system of about 24 satellites can locate anything on Earth within 20 to 300 yards.

A VISIT TO THE SUN

Although it's an average-sized star, the Sun is the largest object in the solar system. It contains about 98 percent of all the solar system's solid material. It's so big more than one million Earths could fit inside. On the surface, the Sun is about 14,000°F

SPOTS AND FLARES

About every 11 years, the Sun develops an unusual number of spots. These dark patches on the Sun's surface are thousands of degrees cooler than the area surrounding them. Near the spots, huge columns of gas called *solar prominences* shoot out dramatically above the surface. Thin columns are called *solar flares*.

▼AURORAS

Sometimes colorful, shimmering curtains of light fill the night sky near the north and south poles. These lights are called *auroras*, caused by radiation from solar flares. Attracted to the magnetism of the Earth, the radiation spirals toward the poles as it approaches.

During a solar eclipse, the Moon passes between the Earth and Sun, blocking all but the outer rim from view.

SOLAR WIND

The Sun is like a huge nuclear furnace, producing incredible amounts of energy and radiation. Blowing out from the *corona*—the outer layer of the Sun—is a stream of particles known as *solar wind*. The wind gusts at 450,000 to 2 million mph, to the far reaches of the solar system.

16

ULYSSES

The probe *Ulysses* was sent off by the *Discovery* shuttle in 1990 to study the Sun. It was the first probe to study the solar system's so-called "third dimension"—above and below the plane in which the planets orbit the Sun.

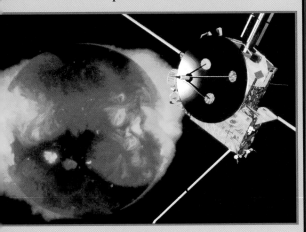

WHOA, H₂0!

Water on the Sun? Believe it or not, in May, 1995, scientists found enough water vapor in a sunspot to fill a lake four square miles in area and 300 feet deep!

SHOOTING STARS

Sometimes pieces of a comet break off. If they enter the Earth's atmosphere, friction causes them to heat up and burn. They are then known as meteors, but are often called "shooting stars."

◀ Carolyn Shoemaker, shown here, with her husband and comet chaser David Levy (at left), has discovered 32 comets. That's more than any living astronomer, and all 32 bear her name.

17

▲ Halley's comet appears in our skies every 76 years and is due to return again in 2061.

DIRTY SNOWBALLS

Made of ice, rock, gas, and dust, *comets* are often called dirty snowballs. They move in orbits that take them close to the Sun, then back to the far reaches of the solar system. As a comet approaches the Sun, the ice vaporizes, and dust and gas are released.

The orbit of Halley's comet is shown here in pink.

THE INNER PLANETS

Between the Earth and the Sun are the only two planets in our solar system that don't have moons. These inner planets are Mercury and Venus. And they are hot! Venus is the hottest planet in our solar system.

FLY-BY SNAPSHOTS

So close to the Sun, Mercury is a difficult body to observe through a telescope. But in March 1974, *Mariner* 10 flew by the planet and photographed its surface. Small, heavily cratered, and airless, Mercury resembles our own Moon. One crater on Mercury is 800 miles wide.

A GODDESS

Venus is named for the Roman goddess of beauty. It is a near twin of the Earth in terms of size. Except for the Sun and Moon, Venus is the brightest object in our sky.

A GOD ▲

The innermost planet, Mercury takes only 88 days to journey around the Sun. Because Mercury appears to Earthlings to be moving very quickly in its orbit, it is named for the Roman wing-footed god.

HIGHS AND LOWS

Without the protection of a gaseous atmosphere, Mercury gets hit hard by the Sun. The temperature can be as hot as 805°F. But the heat is lost at night, as there is no atmosphere to contain it. Then the temperature drops to about -275°F.

OUT OF SIGHT

Also like Earth, Venus is completely covered with clouds. It has an atmosphere. But the air on Venus is mostly carbon dioxide, which would suffocate humans. The cloud cover is 15 miles thick and yellow with sulfuric acid. Like a greenhouse, the clouds trap the Sun's heat and cause temperatures to hang around 900°F.

The *Magellan* probe

Magellan took these photos of Venus as it orbited the planet.

PLANET PEAKS

Spaceship *Magellan* was launched into space by a shuttle in May 1989. It arrived at Venus over a year later and revealed a rugged terrain. The Maxwell Mountains rise to more than 35,000 feet and may be the rim of an ancient volcano. Below they are shown scientifically color enhanced.

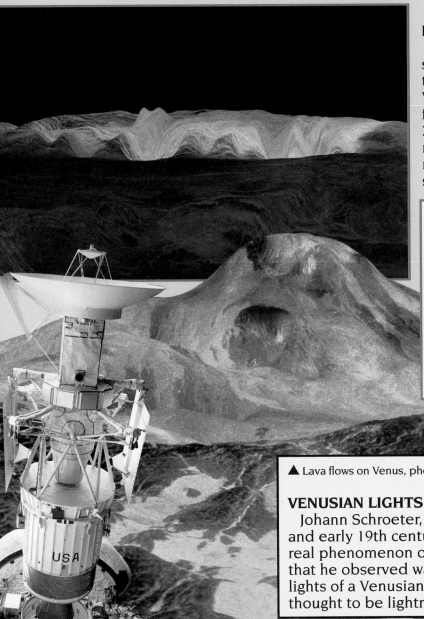

BACKWARDS SPIN ▼

In December 1962, the U.S. spaceship *Mariner* 2 (below) traveled within 21,600 miles of Venus. The exploration confirmed that the planet takes 243 Earth days to *rotate*, or make a complete turn. And it rotates in the direction opposite to Earth—east to west.

▲ Lava flows on Venus, photographed by *Magellan*.

VENUSIAN LIGHTS

Johann Schroeter, who lived in the late 18th and early 19th centuries, was the first to see a real phenomenon on Venus. The "ashen light" that he observed was thought to be the city lights of a Venusian civilization. It is now thought to be lightning.

19

THE RED PLANET

The rusty-red surface of Mars reminded many early observers of a bloody battlefield. The Romans named it after their god of war, and the name is still used today. However, we now know that Mars is red because its soil contains iron that has rusted.

◀ In 1938, actor Orson Wells created a panic when his radio broadcast of *War of the Worlds* was thought to be real news.

MONSTER MOUNTAIN

Although there are no active volcanoes on Mars, the sleeping ones are the tallest yet discovered in our solar system. Olympus Mons rises about 17 miles. That's more than 3 times as tall as Earth's tallest mountain—Mount Everest!

COMMO
CHARACTE

Mars has mo
in common wi
Earth than do
any other plane
Although th
Martian year
almost twice that
Earth's, the Martia
day is only 41 mi
utes longer than a
Earth day. Als
Mars has four se
sons. It has r
running wate
but Mars do
have pol
ice cap

THE ALIEN THREAT

We tend to think of Martians when we think of Mars. Maybe that's because of the science-fiction novel *War of the Worlds*. Written by H.G. Wells in the 19th century, the novel tells of super-intelligent Martians invading the Earth with powerful fighting machines.

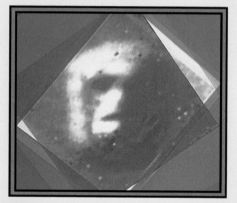

◀ In a photo of Mars's surface, people noticed a strange monkey-face pattern. It reminded them of "the man in the Moon."

MAPPING MARS

[Th]e first [s]pacecraft to [p]ass near Mars, [b]etween 1965 and [19]69, collected data [th]at showed a [cr]atered and lifeless [su]rface. In 1971, the [M]ariner 9 spacecraft [m]apped the whole [pl]anet, revealing a [gr]eat network of [w]aterless [ri]verbeds and [h]uge volca-[no]es.

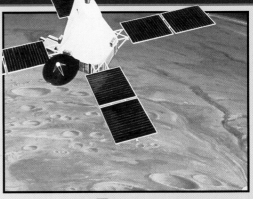

VIKING VICTORY ▶

In 1975, the U.S. launched two *Viking* spacecraft toward Mars. Each had an orbiting module and a landing module. The two *Viking* landers set down on Mars; the *Viking 1 Orbiter* studied the Martian moon called Phobos; and the *Viking 2 Orbiter* surveyed Mars's second moon, called Deimos.

▼ *Viking* preparing to launch.

▼ An asteroid.

A *Viking* lander [ex]ploring Mars.

THE BELT BEYOND

No Martians have visited Earth, but asteroids have. Beyond Mars is the asteroid belt. As large as 600 miles wide, these asteroids orbit the Sun, sometimes crossing Earth's path. If they enter Earth's atmosphere, they are known as *meteors*. If they don't burn up in the atmosphere, they may hit the planet's surface and cause craters.

The largest crater on Earth made by an asteroid is in Arizona. It's 4,150 feet in diameter and about 575 feet deep.

TWO GAS GIANTS

Jupiter and Saturn are the most gigantic planets in our solar system, and they are made mainly of gases. When observing them from space, we see only their atmospheres. But unmanned probes are learning more and more about them.

ROUGH ENTRY ▲

In December 1995, the *Galileo* probe became the first object from Earth to enter Jupiter's atmosphere. After a six-year flight from Earth, *Galileo* penetrated at over 100,000 miles per hour. Before it melted, the unmanned probe relayed a 57-minute weather report to NASA.

From front to back of photo are ▶ Jupiter's planet-sized moons Callistro, Ganymede, Europa, and Io (not shown to scale).

◀ COMET CRASH

When Shoemaker-Lev 9, the comet, passed too close to Jupiter in 1993, the planet's huge gravitational force pulled it even closer. The comet was torn to pieces. About 20 chunks remained in orbit around Jupiter until 1994, when they crashed into the planet. Each crash left a scar on Jupiter.

MANY MOONS

Both Jupiter and Saturn are orbited by many moons—16 are known to Jupiter, and 20 to Saturn. Jupiter's Io is the only moon in our solar system known to have active volcanoes. Ganymede is the largest moon in the solar system.

KING PLANET

The largest planet in our solar system is named for the king of all Roman gods, Jupiter. It's so big that 1,317 Earths could fit inside it. Its gravity is also much greater than Earth's: If you weighed 100 pounds on Earth, you'd weigh 254 pounds on Jupiter.

◄ STRIPES, SPOTS, AND RINGS

The clouds in Jupiter's atmosphere give it a striped appearance. Among the stripes is a huge revolving storm known as the *Great Red Spot*. The spot is three times the size of Earth and was first observed about 300 years ago! The other visible storms known as the *White Ovals* formed in about 1940. When the U.S. *Voyager* spacecraft visited Jupiter in 1979, it discovered there are also rings around the planet. Visible only from the dark side, away from the Sun, the two rings are composed of dark grains of sand and dust.

▲ The *Voyager* spacecraft flew by Jupiter and Saturn, and on to the outermost planets before leaving the solar system.

KING OF RINGS ►

Saturn is the outermost planet visible from Earth with the naked eye. Its most famous feature is its ring system. In 1610, the astronomer Galileo was the first to observe them. There are seven main rings, which are made of ice particles. There are thousands of smaller rings as well, discovered by *Voyager* 1 in 1980.

◄ BIG DADDY

In Roman mythology, Saturn is the father of Jupiter. As a planet, it is nearly as large as Jupiter. But Saturn is not as weighty, having only one-fourth the mass.

THE OUTER LIMITS

The most distant objects in our solar system were unknown to ancient astronomers. They were too far away to see. It took better and better telescopes to find the planets in the outer limits. Uran[us] was sighted in 1781, Neptune in 1846, and Pluto in 1930.

◄ COOL BLUE, RINGS TRUE

A gaseous planet, Uranus i[s] blue-green in appearance and very cool, with atmospheric temperatures a[s] low as -366°F. According to *Voyager* 2, which flew by Uranus i[n] 1986, the planet also has rings. The outer edge of the ring system is located 15,800 miles from the planet'[s] cloud tops.

SIDE ROLL

Being tilted in orbit is not uncommon for planets, but Uranus is almost completely on its side. That means its poles, rather than its equator, point alternately toward the Sun.

SPOT ► AND SCOOTER

A storm rages in the atmosphere of Neptune. This blue planet once had a Great Dark Spot similar to Jupiter's Great Red Spot. But it has recently disappeared. Now another dark spot has appeared to the north, and to the south is a bright cloud, nicknamed "Scooter" because it moves so fast.

▲ Neptune also has rings, verified by *Voyager* 2 in 1989.

PLANET X

Around the turn of the 19th century, astronomer Percival Lowell began looking for what he called "Planet X," far distant in the solar system. He never found X. But, in 1930, 24-year-old Clyde Tombaugh (right) identified the new planet, which became known as Pluto.

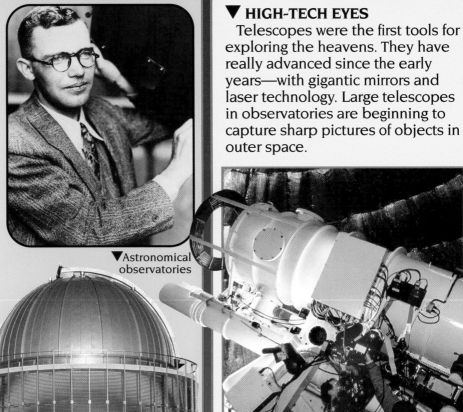

PLUTO EXPRESS

The Hubble Space Telescope has obtained the first clear images of Pluto. But NASA is planning on obtaining even better pictures. In a mission called the Pluto Express, a pair of small spacecraft will study Pluto after the year 2000.

▼ Astronomical observatories

▼ HIGH-TECH EYES

Telescopes were the first tools for exploring the heavens. They have really advanced since the early years—with gigantic mirrors and laser technology. Large telescopes in observatories are beginning to capture sharp pictures of objects in outer space.

◄ CROSSING OVER

Pluto orbits the Sun every 248 Earth years. Having a more oval-shaped orbit, it periodically moves inside Neptune's orbit. It crossed in 1979 and will remain there until 1999.

◄ From left, Uranus, Pluto, and Neptune

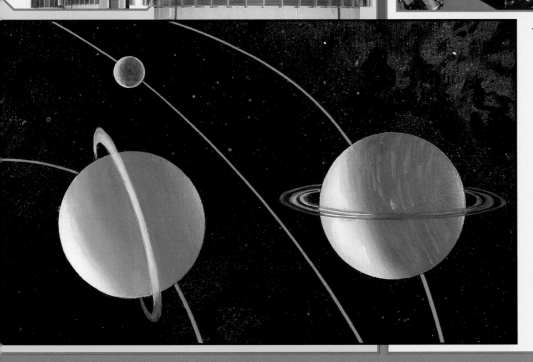

DEEP SPACE

Our galaxy contains as many as 100 billion stars! Like our Sun, they are large, fiery balls of gas. But they don't burn forever. At their hottest, they are blue stars, but eventually they begin to cool down. Stars like our Sun, which is about 5 billion years old, may burn for about 10 billion years.

▼ STAR BIRTH

Stars come in many sizes and live all kinds of lives. They are born in a great cloud of dust and gas called a *nebula*.

From a nebula, stars arise. Gravity tugs at parts of the nebula, and globules develop. These blobs begin to spin faster and faster. As the center reaches about 15 million degrees Fahrenheit, the blob begins to shine and becomes a true star.

GUIDING LIGHT

The stars in our galaxy and the patterns they make stay constant in relation to each other. Since ancient times, they've helped sailors and other travelers navigate. Ancient skywatchers also saw pictures in the patterns of stars. These pictures are called constellations. Today, stars are grouped into 88 constellations. They are used by astronomers to memorize the positions of stars.

The constellation Centaurus.

Some stars form *red super-giants*. These stars can be up to 1,000 times the diameter of our Sun.

If the remains of a star col-lapse into a tight space, a *black hole* may form.

When a huge star dies, it collapses. An explo-sion called a *supernova* occurs.

A super-nova some-times creates a *pulsar*—a spinning ball of matter.

As a star like our Sun runs out of energy, it swells up into a cooler, larger star called a *red giant*.

As it nears death, the core of a star may col-lapse. It then throws off a shell of gas called a *plane-tary nebula*.

At the end of its life, a star like our Sun shrinks to the size of the Earth. Faint but very hot, this star is called a *white dwarf*.

When a white dwarf cools, it becomes a *black dwarf*.

IMAGINATION AND BEYOND

Imagination has always fueled the study and exploration of space. Today, scientists are dreaming of a Moon station, planning trips to Mars and the distant solar system, and searching for life on other planets.

▲ Russian and American astronauts on the Mir.

WORLD MISSIONS

Since 1984, the United States, Canada, Japan, and the European Space Agency have been working toward putting a new space station into orbit. The size of two football fields, this outpost will orbit Earth every 90 minutes with a crew of six.

◀ Astronauts from the U.S. have docked their shuttle on the Russian space station known as Mir. The name Mir means "peace," or "community living in harmony."

ROBOT TO MARS

It weighs only 23 pounds and is about as big as a microwave oven. It's a little robot known as Rocky, and it's expected to answer some big questions about Mars. NASA's robot will analyze the rock and soil on Mars and possibly reveal whether life has ever existed there.

The Russians have developed a Mars robot, too.

NEW PLANETS

Other solar systems have been found at last! One has an ordinary star like our Sun, called Star 51. Orbiting around it is a Jupiter-sized planet. However, it's unlikely the planet has any life. It's positioned so closely to its sun that it probably sizzles at about 1,800° F.

This diagram compares part of our solar system to the three newly discovered solar systems. It shows how close the planets are to their sun.

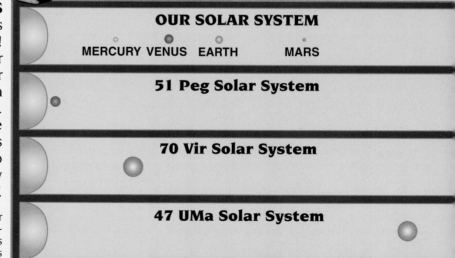

OUR SOLAR SYSTEM

MERCURY VENUS EARTH MARS

51 Peg Solar System

70 Vir Solar System

47 UMa Solar System

GALAXIES GALORE

Edwin Hubble established in the 1920s that our Milky Way is not the only galaxy in the universe. Pictures from the Hubble Space Telescope, which is named for the famous astronomer, have pushed the galaxy count from 10 billion to about 50 billion.

ADVENTURE ON EARTH

Most people don't get a chance to travel beyond Earth. But space adventures can be found right here on the ground. Look for comets passing overhead, like the Hyakutake, which passed over in March 1996. Watch for shooting stars, the phases of the Moon, or a solar eclipse. Space is right overhead!

Imagination rules at this celebration in Hollywood, where a young girl got a chance to meet Neelix and Kazon, characters from *Star Trek Voyager*.

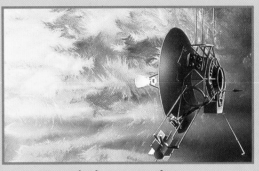

Pioneer 10 was the first spacecraft to leave our solar system.

▲ MESSAGE AWAY

Alien characters often appear in TV and the movies, but do scientists believe that they really exist? Some do. Aboard the two *Voyager* spacecraft sent into space in 1977, there were messages describing life on Earth. Scientists hoped that the two ships might encounter alien civilizations. Who knows? Perhaps someday they will!